VOYAGEUR CLASSICS

BOOKS THAT EXPLORE CANADA

Michael Gnarowski — Series Editor

The Dundurn Group presents the Voyageur Classics series, building on the tradition of exploration and rediscovery and bringing forward time-tested writing about the Canadian experience in all its varieties.

This series of original or translated works in the fields of literature, history, politics, and biography has been gathered to enrich and illuminate our understanding of a multi-faceted Canada. Through straightforward, knowledgeable, and reader-friendly introductions the Voyageur Classics series provides context and accessibility while breathing new life into these timeless Canadian masterpieces.

The Voyageur Classics series was designed with the widest possible readership in mind and sees a place for itself with the interested reader as well as in the classroom. Physically attractive and reset in a contemporary format, these books aim at an enlivened and updated sense of Canada's written heritage.

Y0-AGQ-127

OTHER VOYAGEUR CLASSICS TITLES

The Blue Castle by Lucy Maud Montgomery,
introduced by Dr. Collett Tracey
978-1-55002-666-5

Canadian Exploration Literature: An Anthology,
edited and introduced by Germaine Warkentin
978-1-55002-661-0

Empire and Communications by Harold A. Innis,
introduced by Alexander John Watson
978-1-55002-662-7

The Letters and Journals of Simon Fraser 1806–1808,
edited and introduced by W. Kaye Lamb, foreword by Michael Gnarowski
978-1-55002-713-6

Maria Chapdelaine: A Tale of French Canada by Louis Hémon,
translated by W.H. Blake, introduction and notes by Michael Gnarowski
978-1-55002-712-9

Mrs. Simcoe's Diary by Elizabeth Posthuma Simcoe,
edited and introduced by Mary Quayle Innis, foreword by Michael Gnarowski
978-1-55002-768-6

Selected Writings by A.J.M. Smith,
edited and introduced by Michael Gnarowski
978-1-55002-665-8

VOYAGEUR CLASSICS

BOOKS THAT EXPLORE CANADA

IN THIS POEM I AM

SELECTED POETRY OF ROBIN SKELTON

INTRODUCED AND EDITED BY HAROLD RHENISCH

DUNDURN PRESS

TORONTO

Editor: Michael Carroll
Copy-editor: Marja Appleford
Designer: Erin Mallory
Printer: Marquis

Library and Archives Canada Cataloguing in Publication

Skelton, Robin, 1925-1997.
    In this poem I am : selected poetry of Robin Skelton / edited and introduced by Harold Rhenisch.

ISBN 978-1-55002-769-3

    I. Rhenisch, Harold, 1958- II. Title.

PS8537.K38A17 2007   C811'.54   C2007-904677-0

1 2 3 4 5   11 10 09 08 07

**Conseil des Arts
du Canada**

**Canada Council
for the Arts**

**ONTARIO ARTS COUNCIL
CONSEIL DES ARTS DE L'ONTARIO**

Canada

We acknowledge the support of the **Canada Council for the Arts** and the **Ontario Arts Council** for our publishing program. We also acknowledge the financial support of the **Government of Canada** through the **Book Publishing Industry Development Program** and **The Association for the Export of Canadian Books**, and the **Government of Ontario** through the **Ontario Book Publishers Tax Credit program**, and the **Ontario Media Development Corporation**.

Care has been taken to trace the ownership of copyright material used in this book. The author and the publisher welcome any information enabling them to rectify any references or credits in subsequent editions.

J. Kirk Howard, President

Printed and bound in Canada.
Printed on recycled paper.
www.dundurn.com

Dundurn Press	Gazelle Book Services Limited	Dundurn Press
3 Church Street, Suite 500	White Cross Mills	2250 Military Road
Toronto, Ontario, Canada	High Town, Lancaster, England	Tonawanda, NY
M5E 1M2	LA1 4XS	U.S.A. 14150

For Sylvia

CONTENTS

A PORTRAIT OF THE POET AS A BOOK:
AN INTRODUCTION BY HAROLD RHENISCH

In a country in which poetry has been largely a private and apologetic pursuit, Robin Skelton played the part of the poet with grand style: flowing beard, a mane of white hair, rings on every finger, a huge amulet around his neck, all topped off with a black hat that looked as if it came from a gondolier in Venice but really was picked up at the re-enactment of a Cariboo Gold Rush–era general store in Barkerville in the British Columbia Interior. Robin Skelton looked as if he was onstage. He was.

Skelton's intellectual reputation was equally eclectic: scholar of the Irish Renaissance, artist, witch, art collector, novelist, storyteller, spellmaker, surrealist, anthologist, poet, editor, husband, translator, father, exorcist, lover, reviewer, shaman, friend, chain-smoking rescuer of drowning bottles of Jameson's Irish Whiskey, scryer, teacher. It would all be dauntingly incongruous, except that Robin Skelton came from an age in the world when scholars were conversationalists, able through their familiarity with the tradition to see patterns where others did not and, above all, to bring ideas and people together. Skelton's first act as a poet and an intellectual was to make the man we knew as Robin Skelton. That man was the delivery vehicle — the human equivalent of a book — for an entire world.

The book, Robin Skelton, however, was a man of contradictions. He lived for the innovative, the philosophical, and the new — after all, his poetic roots were in surrealism — but he did so as a nineteenth-century man of letters, not a twentieth-century one. He let his hair and beard grow for twenty-five years, too, untrimmed, like a Welsh Samson — not as a countercultural protest, but because, without any McLuhanesque "the-medium is the message" fuss, he believed in embodying, not discussing, his ideas and beliefs. And he was generous about it.

In the same way the alchemist John Dee fled the political intrigues of the sixteenth-century London court to set up the greatest library in England in the seclusion of goosey, rural Margate, Robin Skelton left the funereal academic world of Manchester to live in a big old house in Oak Bay, British Columbia, which he turned into a shrine to poetry and art. Actually, it was more an alchemical diagram of the human heart than a house in any recognizable sense, with mystery novels stacked up in the kitchen, ghost stories in the haunted back bedroom, sagging shelves of humour in the loo, goddesses (rescued from flea markets) spilling off the mantel and encroaching on the living room, modernist paintings covering every conceivable inch of wall space, and one of the world's best collections of Irish poetry on the somewhat spiralling stairs leading to the second storey where oak and apple trees knocked at the windows. Within this magical chamber and propelled by it into the world, Robin Skelton was larger than life, a man who read his poetry to all comers in a sonorous voice honed with the British Broadcasting Corporation and who opened his house weekly to ply an entire city with wine in celebration of art. He was a university.

More privately, Robin Skelton was a healer of broken bones, a revenant releasing ghosts from the pain that kept them on this earth, and a celebrant who brought children to the world by the touch of his hands. In short, in a provincial world too small for his horizons, he played the alchemist, like John Dee to Queen Elizabeth I, promising through his dedication to bring all human pursuits into one unified vision — a vision, ironically, almost completely lost through the vicissitudes of a changing world that eventually left him on the margins of his art. In the end, much like John Dee, who died in penury and obscurity, or even like the homunculus Shakespeare made of him, Prospero himself, Robin Skelton, who spoke for the entirety of the English tradition, the direct heir of David Gascoyne, Dylan Thomas, Robert Graves, T.S. Eliot, and the occasional tradition of A.E. Housman and John Masefield, compatriot of Ted Hughes, John Montague, Tony Connor, and W.S. Graham, died quietly and frustrated in a small Canadian city isolated even from Canada — his books increasingly unread and his passions increasingly out of fashion, lost to both his English and his Canadian readers by his firm insistence on uniting both traditions in a world which had other, more angular interests.

It was not, however, the end. At his death Robin Skelton left (not unexpectedly) ten unpublished manuscripts, ranging from poetry to fiction, from ghost stories to journals and histories. This bridger of worlds, to whom every act could be apprehended through words, also left a legacy of attention to the musicality of words, one that appears to be becoming more contemporary again as mainstream poetry's infatuation with Marxism increasingly wanes and a new generation of Canadian and American poets turns to classical models. There is much for them in Skelton's quixotic attempts to heal poetry's civil war, to renew a still-living tradition by merging it with anti-metrical modernism. Even though growing insularity dogged Skelton through his three and a half decades in Canada, after two generations of intensified specialization, many Canadian poets are now returning to the gregariousness of classicism — yet they are doing so largely without the benefit of either Skelton's eclectic imagination or his experience at adapting those forms to the Canadian experience. Sadly, Robin Skelton's life eclipsed his art.

To help right this wrong, I have assembled here a sampling of Skelton's poetry. In the following pages, you will find some of his signature effects: iambic pentameters broken in half, and sometimes in half again, to invigorate the short-line free-verse forms of the

1970s; resurrected verse forms; newly minted verse forms modelled after the intricacies of Welsh prosody; long experience of rhyme and repetitive verse structures applied to the ever-seductive and ever-fragmented Canadian long poem; the half rhymes of Irish tradition applied as poultices to bind poems together for ears unused to harder accents; a resurrection of Anglo-Saxon as a primary poetic language; a perennial insistence that the universal can be found in the intimate; and the personal example that true conservatism is not a reactionary force but one that embraces all traditions.

Such constructivist tendencies had, obviously enough, little place in the deconstructivist world of Canadian poetry from the 1960s to the 1990s — and as small as that place was to begin with, Robin Skelton made it even smaller by his own continual, repeated efforts to write over and over again the one collection of poems that was his life. In the end, he published over sixty collections of this poetry, most of them identical in shape and chock full of poems eschewing large philosophical gestures for small, intimate ones concerned increasingly with family, friends, and a Wiccan philosophy completely at odds with the way most people in the Western world have come to think and live. With a romantic flourish, Skelton insisted that it was not his job, as a poet, to select from this output; it was his job to write, just as it was the job of a scryer to see within a crystal ball and the task of the critics to select. It was a gesture grandly disconnected from the realities of contemporary literature, in which critics have increasingly developed their own creative and analytical traditions. Critics such as Robin Skelton — the collector, the host of Thursday night open houses on Victoria Avenue — may have done work like that, but then he was, as Ezra Pound wrote of himself two generations before, "out of step with his time."

It is as a reader, then as a student, and finally as a working poet and friend that I grew to know Robin Skelton and have made this (no doubt imperfect) selection. In doing so, I have tried to present the one book Skelton was trying to write, which appears in pieces throughout his collected works. It is the story of an emblematic world, the eternal tapestry of a goddess and a stag-horned god, of life coming to consciousness from the earth and returning to the earth, to trees, water, fire, and air. It is a pre-Christian, pre-scientific, pre-intellectual philosophy in which words are not signifiers of thought but spells that call up the power of the earth, an alchemical vision that attempts to stand still at a point at which the world of the saints and the world of the enlightenment remain unsundered, in which a poem can be at the same time a highly academic act, an exploration of individuality, and a work of magic with real effects on a real world. There are poems of "high" and "low" art here, as well as spells and prayers, meditations, a shamanic map or two, and in the centre of the book, "messages," those strange, inspired, angelic "gifts" at the core of Skelton's art, which he received in the seven years from 1962 to 1969. In making the selection for this volume, I have held to the image that Skelton's themes repeat like the ripples of water spreading out from a pebble (the messages) dropped into a pool (his life) and have attempted to bring together the best ripple from each dropped pebble. I have also held to Skelton's method of presenting poems out of temporal sequence, because to a man who believed that we remain eternal and unchanging from birth to death while the poetry changes under our hands, any imposition of temporal order on a poetic production that can only be understood in its entirety would negate its ultimately human message, and Skelton's message is, paramountly, profoundly and contagiously human. I hope that readers coming to this work will discover what Robin Skelton's students and readers and the poets and artists of Victoria, British Columbia, have known for decades — that for all of his personal and poetic idiosyncracies one of the world's true poets lived among us for a time and gave us his heart.

I

WATCHING THE HOUSE MOVE

THE HOUSE

This is the house
in which the words

are walls, are furniture,
are doors and cushions,

and in which the paintings,
chairs and rugs

are words, and all the words
stand in a circle

round the changing moment.
But when you enter,

opening the rhetoric
of the door,

seeing round you
vocabularies of sculpture,

libraries of sound,
do not assume

this is exclusively
a house of language;

think rather that it is
a place where love

has struggled to discover
what it means

and made these words
to hold you till it knows.

FLUX

Moving between
continents of sea,
the earth heaves, ripples,
rises, falls,
presents a mountain
that becomes a deep,
shifts in its colouring,
green to gold to bronze,
swells and diminishes,
as the seas remain
changelessly themselves,
responding only
to the steady
tugging of the moon,
the sliding of the wind.
How can one chart
the hills and forests
in their constant change,
how set a course
from valley into valley
when the seasons move
the very earth
one travels as one travels,
and how find
a steady anchorage
in these heaving hills?

There is no settled
anchorage or haven.
As I watch, a house-beam
crumbles, falls,
a tree thrusts rock apart,
a mountain slides
a hundred houses down
into brown clay
and flame chars half a
green-clad county black,
and there's no certainty.
The child we knew
is now a man we do not
care to know,
and he that killed our fathers
calls us friend.
What is identity?
The man I was
walks through these words I write,
his alien eyes
accusing me; the man
I may become
stands in the doorway
mocking what I say.

IN THIS POEM I AM

And in this poem I am,
Whoever else I am.
          — W.S. Graham, *The Dark Dialogues*

First Poem

In this poem I am
someone you meet outside
the public library. He
is carrying a small book
which he has not yet read.
His hands are blue with cold.
He tells you his wife is buying
new drapes for the winter.

He is not important.
You do not have to mind
anything that he says.
It is only talk
to make smoke of the breath.
He stamps his feet. It is
November in Oak Bay.
Even the trees are shuddering.

In this poem I am
making smoke of the breath.
It shows me I am saying
something. What it is
does not matter. All
that always only matters
is what we have still to learn
and that we try to speak

to each other still
in spite of the bitter cold
frosting the fallen browns
of leaves in an Oak Bay
that only differs from
your other place in being
where we meet and chat,
together in this poem
to stamp our feet and clutch
the books we have not yet read.

Second Poem

In this poem I am
walking through Beacon Hill Park.
The pond is frozen. Ducks
are walking upon the ice,
shuddering their blacks and greens.
A woman in fur-lined boots
is casting crumbs. A dog
is walking on its own.

You want the other poem?
The one in which I am
the voice of God? I think
it is too cold for that.
I have just come in
from the fine chill of the park.
Wait a moment while
I put the coffee on

and clear my throat. It is
a poem I do not like
to live in very much.
I get a little deaf
listening to those words
that God might overhear,
and though He understands
the fix that I am in

I shouldn't push my luck.
Can't I say in this poem
I am the way you sit
expectant in that chair,
your legs crossed and your hand
upon your rocking knee,
hoping for something good?
I hope for something good.
Almost I found it there
walking in Beacon Hill Park.

Third Poem

In this third poem I am
someone you expect.
I hear you say "At last!"
I guess I ought to blush
but only stamp off snow
and lay my boots aside.
Your room is dark and warm.
I don't know who you are.

This is the usual thing.
I guess you'll understand
that when I come myself
I'm often rather shy
and clumsy with my feet.
Don't put away the cat.
There's no need for a fuss.
I'm sure my welcome's warm.

In this poem I am
at least no sad surprise,
familiar at least.
You've heard it all before
a number of good times
(I hope the times were good).
Your face is rather flushed.
Perhaps I'm not quite right?

Well, we all make mistakes.
I mean not to be more
or less than you expect,
but often there's a change
between the knock (or ring)
and greeting who comes in.
I always come in slow;
it gives time to adjust
as we (shall we?) adjust.
You must know what I mean.

BACK AGAIN

Themes of return obsess me.
I've come back
so often that the half smile,
puzzled stare,
and cautious recognition
are become
the way for me to recognize myself
as being what I am,
a revenant
only a little changed
by changing times.

Surprise is muted now.
You're back again!
Lost weight! How have you been?
They don't ask where
which may be just as well.
How could I answer?
Paphlagonia? Paramnesia? Hell?
I guess I'd tell them
Just the usual places,
nowhere different,
as if they knew,
as I do not,
those fly-specks on the map,
the black lines and the blue,
the stains and names.

Yet maybe I should try
to spell it out,
like answering the perfunctory
How are you?
with details of disorder,
loss of breath,
and muscle stiffening,
tell them I have been
a different man;
I have to say a man
because it's hard to think
myself a thing
and *thing*'s the wrong word anyway.
Let's say
I've been a different thought
a different time

and wait for questions
that won't come, or if
they do will be
unanswerable. I
don't speak this language
when I speak of that.
I do not know what language
I should speak.
Maybe there is none.
I was kept quite busy.
There was always everything to do.
I tell you, it is real good
to be back.
That at least's an accurate
obvious lie

which they may get, or not.
Who cares? I think
sometimes there is no future
in renewal,
as there is no past;
it is all here,
as I am here,
my elsewhere in my eyes,
my hands, my tongue,
the blinding of the light.
I wipe my glasses
and accept a drink
in comradeship,
as if we were all comrades,
as if they had not been
away themselves.

BURNING STICKS, MALLORCA

for Anthony Kerrigan

Poems should be wisdom
or be love.
       I burn
dry sticks to incense
that this orchard hill
may blossom rich, fruit heavy,
fill the Spring
with radiance, and the belly
with good meat.
It is enough to labour
if with trust
in wholeness of the earth
and gods, (or God),
setting the furrow
or remaking words,
carving the ancient olive wood,
or, hunched
above clay, giving spirit
simple forms —
king, soldier, angel, bull.
Each man must turn
what is into what is
or he will die
as buildings die
left tenantless and soiled
beside forgotten fields.
Beyond this bay
sea stretches to the first
names of our world,
the broken images

of moon and sun,
hoarded and crumbling,
and yet what was done
remains a frame for learning
and for thought.
The fence-posts round this olive grove
are wrought
as phalluses;
this white clay figurine,
(crowned, virile, potent,
fresh as earliest dawn),
is one of those
that only virgins may
create to plead fruition,
and the play
of bull and man still wounds
the timeless sky.
Time is the earth's
most ample perfidy.

Poems should be timeless
and of time.
     We change
little but names
and accidents.
     We fall
upon one earth
and with one mouth applaud
one harvest
and cry one cry of despair.

Poems should be timeless
and be love.
          They prove
little but movements
of the hearts they move,
concerned to celebrate
not spell the truth.
The love that puts
this message in my mouth
may be my own
but is not mine alone.
The smoke of incense
rises from the stone
by my intent
but not by my own will;
it is the will of being's self
that fills
the crowding blossom
with the gentle haze
and asks the mountains
for their certainties.

LIMITS

Everywhere there are limits,
barriers, boundaries,
shorelines, rivers, ditches,
fenceposts, crossings
that one must not cross,
foods one can't eat,
and even words one dare not
speak. This earth
is parcelled out among us
and each man
must live within his
portion. This is mine.
You're welcome to
explore it, as I do,
continually.
                 Here's
my apple tree,
and here wife, daughter, dog,
and over there
a group of ghosts
not speaking to each other
but by way of me,
and, up beyond
that red brick house,
a copse, a pool, a broken
white horse lying on
harsh concrete, snapped
off at the thigh.
Why don't you look around,
see for yourself?

I see for myself now,
and it's a great
improvement upon seeing
just for other people
who can't see
(they say) without me,
though they'll have to learn,
as I have, through the years,
that there are limits
upon sharing
as on pain and love
and understanding,
not to mention time,
which I am always mentioning
like a clock
that makes the round trip
of its boundaries over,
over, over, over,
till it stops
at one fencepost for ever.
I don't know
where I would soonest
stop, but all too soon
I know I'll have to,
stilled within my limits
that won't feel like
limits any more,
but crossings that one crosses,
words one speaks.

MARIGOLDS

Eyes fading now,
I look on marigolds

clustered orange-yellow
by the fence,

hardy and handsome.
In our big allotment

behind the apple trees
of the vicarage garden

I planted marigolds;
they spread like crazy,

hot to the eye,
as was the sun that summer,

the clay soil baked and cracked,
the little pebbles

shiny and hot to fingers,
and my father

grumped about them.
"Weeds," he said, "just weeds,"

but there was no way
we could get them out

short of pick-axes or,
maybe, explosives;

and they were there to stay,
and stay they did

as these will stay
as long as I have strength

to keep untidy splendours
in this place

I need for vision
and for learning how

to burn the neat dead answers
from my mind.

II
A FAMILY LIFE

KINSHIP
for John Pass

Kin, Kinship, Kindred....
The look of the words
bothers my head;

that angled beginning,
that whistle-thin
second comer, that n,

a small door, narrow
to hooped shoulders,
give me a shudder

I can't shake off. It's
a stone-hacked hut
the ninth century built

on a dank headland,
a lean shrill child,
and a man with a sword;

it's a scooped cavern
in rotting sandstone
where guns have driven

the sparse survivors
of indian wars;
and it is a house

lit by one candle,
the Cross twisted
to hate on the threshold,

yet these words bring
warmth, safety, things
that haunt our old songs

of the terrible need
for a gift-bearing tide,
a sharing of dread,

and something I can't
put a phrase to yet
that, clenched as a fist,

hate, envy, pain,
lust, cannot distrain —
the last thing we own.

PRAYER BEFORE BIRTH

I cannot pray for myself.
Only just can I bear to ask
for words which are not for me
but for the grinders and yellow tusks
of this creature to crack,
crush, and make paste;
I don't know what he is,
but the tracks where he has passed
smell hot and rank. I do not
pray to the gods but to him,
the malignant judge, the sweltering heart,
the brute reason.

And pray for you,
though not to get you words,
but different blessings
like muscles that are lean and hard,
eyes that are clear, teeth sound,
four fingers and a thumb on each hand,
and only one head.
I ask that you have
strength delicacy and innocence in love
often satisfied on a firm bed,
and a good thirst, a strong hunger,
in the appetite passion, in the mind order.

I ask also the creature to whom these words
are addressed and to whom they fall
that he may remember my devotion, the bared
flagellant back, the hairshirt, the clumsy cowl,

41

and, leaving my pellets of skin and split bone
on your step,
breathing with breath I gave him,
rear and rip
down all your failures, giving you the intent
lost desperate courage that alone
is worth prayer or defilement.

THE WAKING

Tonight's my birth-night. I can't sleep. One leg
twitches and jerks. It was broken at the thigh
when I was born, and now it has remembered.
The body thinks chronology aside

and 2 a.m. casts lendings off. I turn,
bullying the springs, resentfully to mutter
at that limb's dull ache, as I resent,
all too often, the stiffening of another

that remembers farther darker acts,
casting the mind out gasping. Wide awake,
I rise, walk through the house. My children sleep,
steering through dreams and accidents that come back

always to man and womanhood, trapped, staring,
on such a night as this, at shaking blind,
faint shadowed ceiling, sightless dangling bulb,
with thinking body and with helpless mind.

AUTOBIOGRAPHY

We all were born in nineteen twenty five;
mother became mother then, and father father,
and the village a real village with real houses,
and people letting smoke from the chimney tops.
The cows in the field found cowness, the big tree
got its size back, and held up the sky.
The birds flew high, because they'd just learnt how to,
and the stairs began to climb, the roof to guard.

Everything started then. We went on together,
getting used to it, getting used to our eyes
and the noises we made, and the fingers made for something
fiddly but rather uncertain, and moving around,
getting space straight, too: in volume X
nothing bigger than X can get, and doors that open
one way won't stay shut if you treat them wrong,
and some things are much harder than other things.

Well, we got it learnt, in a sort of fashion.
Two of us thought we knew a bit already,
and had to unlearn it all, to learn it true;
I was starting from scratch, and got on alright.

At least for a time. Then things began to stop.
The village turned into cardboard on odd days,
and the cows were in the way, and the sycamore tree
dropped dead flies in my hair and dwindled; so
it went on, just like that. We'd started right.
Everything started together for us that year.
Then, bit by bit, things stopped. Some new things started.
Balls began bouncing, for instance, and books to talk,

and wheels to turn and pens to write and blot,
and hands to grab, and violins to play,
and things are still beginning. But the dead.
Oh how the stockstill stopped lives stand about.
Now over thirty years we've seen them stiff.
Only on good days one or two have moved
hesitantly, started up again.
But mostly not. Till now. And now, well now
we suddenly start again. He started us —
I as father, she as mother, they
the same again and different. The house
has proper walls and doors, the chimneys smoking
real smoke up into a proper sky,
where birds have found what voices can get said,
and trees have got the job to keep them there,
and eyes begin to learn the way to look,
and ears to listen, and our hands, our hands,
oh all our hands find that they're here for something
fiddly, uncertain perhaps, but must hold on.

LAND WITHOUT CUSTOMS
for John Montague

My land had no customs. Habits, tricks
of the slow tongue, leading beasts to grass,
roads slape with rain, or answering
weddings and deaths in a dry voice
scurfy as dust in the village square,
boys' names carved into the old stocks,

these — but no customs. Unless you count
the old men making one stretch of wall
the place for their backs, spring sun
blinking their eyes; or the way all
was marbles one day, the next tops
in the road alongside the brick school.

Certain inevitables there were: the rub
of hands on apron at house door
to speak to strangers, the mild horse
surging the plough at a harsh roar
of ritual violence, the long silence
before speech. And these were
known and unknown. The land stood
somewhere inside them. A phrase missed,
a nod too easy, and boots dragged
at embarrassed cobbles. Two miles west
it was shallower, lighter. I once saw
a man there run for the town bus.

But no customs. In a way stronger
for that, I think. There was no need
to assert the place. It grew, changed;

the electric came and a new road
out to the south, and the telephone.
The pump was condemned. But the past stood.

And I daresay still, in its own way,
stands. Though a plaque by the old stocks
set in the wall is a thought strange,
there in the square are the old looks,
the pause before speech, the drab men
spitting in dust. Should I go back

these will have made me. The small fields
are as small elsewhere, the sky as blue
or just as grey with a thread of rain,
the stacks as lumpish, but here grew
something inalienable, a way
of giving each least thing its due,

a rock to living. A land without
customs, yes, but a land held
hard on its course, unsparing, firm
in its own ways. As I grow old
time hardens into that sure face
watching the foreign, shiftless world.

THE CIRCUMCISION

Smell the nice scent, she said. The table slithered
under my back on the blanket. I was ashamed
as I had been taught to be ashamed. The Doctor
held sweetness to my nose until the ceiling
swam and buckled, became a mist, sea-mist
shifting over the details of the mind,
and voices gathered distance. From far off
a small sharp pain pierced what I must not touch,
and my gut contracted. Half awake,
I shivered to the brutal, soothing words.

Cracks on the ceiling mapping a country of mist,
a snowscape stained by yellowing smears of time,
what should hurt, hurt.
             The tangible shame came home
suddenly, bandaged, ludicrous, alarming.
It was a *thing*. (There were no words to use
except the disallowed.) A *thing* was hurting,
a nameless shameful *thing*, a *thing* I mustn't
see in a mirror, show to anyone, mention,
but only use, of necessity, on my knees
above the equally nameless shining porcelain
vivid with bluebirds on the rim, pink breasted,
wide-winged, wide-beaked, flying ...
             Wide-beaked, flying,
I lay in the mists of my bed to the sound of the sea
and the distant spectral voices. I flew. I faltered.
Gradually round my bed the shapes of air
solidified: my mother, her nurse-faced sister,
pulling the bedclothes back.

He isn't crying
but singing! (my mother's voice) *He's only singing.*
You're only singing, aren't you? I sang my crying,
hearing the tension twang in her throat, the laughter
of something frightened nearing, the eyes like
      gimlets,
and stitch by stitch by stitch and shame by shame,
the ceiling a sheeted mirror, the door concealment,
the curtains clogging the sky, the song explained
my loyalty to her terror, and cried my own.
I wept my terror. Then everything slowly, slowly
altered its dark perspectives. Upon my knees
I saw shame hurt for being shameful, pitied
what I could not love, nor yet protect,
and, mirrored back in urine, watched my features
shift and shiver, cramped upon my knees
praying to something other than the God
I knew from bedtime and the blur of sleep,
something nameless, vivid, mortal — someone
accepting the strange sweet smell, the ceiling
      buckling,
the twisting shapes in the air, not Mother or Father,
but what has been always nameless, private, holy,
the shaming of shame by the human, the peace of
      the wound
discovered, the mirror transforming,
      but singing not crying.

ALISON JANE SKELTON
Aged One

This infant staggerer carries round
in clutched fist doll and animal —
splayed ragged arms and flayed face,
chewed wet fur, torn paws. Her falls
are sudden squats on the claimed ground,
her lunges trials of guessed space.

Triumphant tyranny in her clutch
and huge cry shakes us to the heart;
the clenched assertion of her stare
and random language tugs apart
each easy sentiment; her pink
fat hands grub realistic floors.

Small pities have no place in her,
love a demand, intolerant, plain,
for food or service; tears dried,
withdrawn into her own again,
she tramples doll and animal
strewn carelessly across the wide

expanse of all the place she knows.
Can years bring alteration here,
or will she, in her private strength
of woman, keep this hidden near,
unknown of watcher, listener, friend,
or conquering lover, till, at length,

necessity and will combine
in summoning her to wake again
the pitiless tyrannic bent
of her own self-absorbment? Then,
will she be strong, who, small, is strong,
and force life to replenishment?

A SON SLEEPING
for Nicholas

So far, so good. I daren't commit myself
to anything more certain, but so far
it's pretty good, would set me up for life
if I weren't wise to how life knocks you down.
Anyway, I'm here. And he. We both. Together.
Compact in one another at this time.
He has a look of me, same dragged down mouth.
Maybe the same kink brings the same distress.
No matter. Time will tell. But time has tolled
its bells too loud for me, now fingers ring
the changes of a fatherhood. He'll drive
his plough above the bones of my quick dead.

It's to be expected. We expect,
by destiny bound, each man to stand above
the cradle with his epitaph to hand,
while hands that rock the cradle learn to rule
out any copybook and only pray
Gentle upon him be your hands, my God,
always your presence; let him not believe
and doubt together; let him not attempt
the reasoned emptiness, the cleansing mind.

So far it's easy. Keep your pecker up.
Retain the casual lightness of this tone.
Joke a little. Innocent and flesh,
he sleeps his paradox while you unsolve
the ready answers, tracing each truth back
to how his first stare told you all's unknown.
And all is still unknown. It would be good

52

to stand aside and pay the moral out
into the labyrinth someone else explores
but, unfortunately, that can't be done,
the thread lost, rotten, frayed, too short by half,
and I half wish I'd let the whole thing drop.

But not *him*. No. I think it's clear he is,
and, being, is as much as time my way
and my existence. I can only hope
he has strong children without facing death.
May he be strong as animals are strong,
and kind and gentle, not think overmuch
of where we are. So I would disinherit
my next days from his companionship
to save him finding my way into … hell?

Hell is a big word, but I'll let it stay.
To see and find is to fear dark and loss,
and we are mortal. There's the nub, my son.
You have brought death in your two fumbling hands.
And life, of course. It makes one see how God,
(if it were God), was God in being born.
This birth brings God to me, is God perhaps,
renewing, altering, transforming death.
Now I've succeeded. Something has got out.
Words in a pattern. Thoughts upon a string.

So far, so good. I can't get farther now.
Words have walked out on me. This quiet end
of every exploration at the centre

of the labyrinth must wait for truth,
(if truth there is), must wait in presence of
a doubt and a belief and all my love
held in his fingers. Love is the last word.
To love is mortal, and death stirs at love.

TRIPTYCH

1

My deaf and peering mother
crazy with age
mumbles her supper.

She knows I am not
her growing son.
I'm too old for that.

When she is gone
he'll be left helpless.
She wants to go home.

Her home is with us?
We are talking nonsense.
She is angry at lies.

She hangs onto the handle
of the back door
clutching her bundle,

a crumpled letter, a crust
in a folded napkin.
It is England or bust.

2

My bent blind mother
deafened by time
hunches her walker.

She means to get
to the front room chair.
There she will sit

without a word.
She has managed it
although it was hard.

Is there anything more?
What would she like?
She does not answer.

It is enough
to have made no mistake.
She has altered life.

3

My white-haired mother
clutching her blanket
is crying out,

O help me God.
She has lost her wits
remembering the dead

who cannot come
and the sisters she had.
She is lost, alone.

It is two in the morning.
Where is her son?
Will he be coming?

I say I am here.
Her arms are thin.
What else must she bear?

The pillow is soft.
There is nothing to fear
and some time left.

HERITAGE

With a kind of cough
and a cloud of dust,
(brown snuff of seventy
patient years),
the front of the old hotel
ripped away;
packed boxes papered red
and blue and green
and flaked with blistered
paint remain for less
than half an hour,
then everything is gone
but the crook-limbed
garry oak, the fir,
the monkey-puzzle,
and the huddled laurel.

The glass (late art nouveau)
was taken out,
and the porcelain tiles
sold to a dealer
down on Johnson Street,
but the new apartments
will be labelled Heritage
in gold,
and occupied in part
by ladies who
were born around the year
the place was built.

Heritage is a thing
we understand
only when we are losing it
like marriage;
it is what we know
we cannot keep
faith with save by sad
nostalgic acts
of fantasy, recalling
in a shred
of handkerchief,
a faded photograph,
events to which they never
did belong,
and, anyway, whose values
we distrust.

Such is our need and
custom. I myself
have kept my father's
battered old tin hat
and his bandolier,
his ribboned medals.
Someday they'll go —
maybe when I am dead,
or perhaps, some weekend,
wearying of history,
I'll clean house, take them
down to Johnson Street,
or put them up for auction
as collectibles.

Or will my children
call them Heritage?
My mother taps her way
around the house
remembering only that she
should remember,
peering, wondering who,
and what, and where,
much as I do,
lumbering through these rooms,
picking up old books,
collectors' items,
discovered in an
after-luncheon daze
of Beaujolais some place
in Johnson Street
where they'll end up again.
Ambition dreams
of permanence in what we
find to love,
and choices, when they're made,
are planned as final.
That patch of torn blue paper
in the rubble
was surely once well-chosen,
in good taste,
expensive, even envied,
as am I
envied, they tell me,
gossipy with drink
in the beer parlour
just off Johnson Street,

for this old stately house
in which I write,
but it won't stand for ever;
when it's gone
will its replacement be
called Heritage?
And my replacement —
what will they call that?
I know myself the more
the more I age
and begin to lose
what I must lose —
taste, hearing, sight, and,
gradually, mind.
I envy those that pull
the houses down
for they at least leave nothing
to hang onto,
no weight upon their backs
of fear and loss,
no guilt, no desperate memories;
they renew
earth's innocence, and yet
I guess their houses,
too, hold photographs,
those quiet ghosts
that stare out with their
half-remembered eyes
at what they've left us
as our heritage.

HOUSE TOUR

This is the room I died in.
They thought it a pleasant room,
but the windows were always too bright
for the grey fog in my eyes.
I had to keep closing the shutters
against the sun and, too,
against the bothersome faces
of young girls looking in.

They none of them saw the girls,
Lily, Sarah, Jane,
and sometimes Grace. It wasn't
kind of them to intrude
again like that. I wanted
almost to quite forget,
or remember in my own way.
My own way was the way

I'd lived for the longest time,
and who could expect me to change?
This is the kitchen. I used
to put the dishes away
when the dishwasher had finished,
but I got it wrong
too often and had to stop.
It's hard to stop like that.

Along here is the hall.
I walked here near the end
with a stupid sort of frame.
They fretted that I might fall.

Sometimes I did. But I
had been falling for thirty years.
It wasn't any different
except that I couldn't get up.

And now the front room. That
is where he would always sit,
the man who wasn't my son
but spoke as if he was,
and may have been sometimes
in his more gentle voice.
I think it made him cross
to see the bitter end.

I only know one more room.
I didn't go upstairs.
No, don't go in. It isn't
decent to show it off.
There was where I had
to come to terms with things
I'd rather not discuss.
They took away the lock.

I think that's about all,
except for the little place
between the inner door
and the door that leads outside.
I struggled a good bit here.
I wanted to get on home.
They said it was far away,
as if I didn't know that!

It was very far away
and they were always near.
I never liked people near;
I kept myself to myself
all the years. I taught
my son to think like that.
Paddle your own canoe
is what his father sang,

and I was paddling my own
canoe in a kind of way,
trying to do it at least.
Independent all
of us girls were at home.
Did I tell you about home?
I'm not sure where it was,
but it was never here,

never, never, never.
Now it is time to rest.
I used to rest a lot.
I couldn't read or hear
most of what went on.
You can go away.
I don't want any dinner,
and I won't go to bed.

LANDMARKS

I

Discoveries recur
and are ephemeral;
they happen, startle, vanish
as a mist
lifts suddenly upon
an unknown headland,
rocks, trees, watchers,
and, as quick, descends.

I pick a pebble from the
beach; the pebble
first is miracle
and then is stone.

Discovery is the transient
only freedom:
we are released, unknown,
to the unknown,
and altered by renewal
of the first
significant astonishment
of breath:
here is an island
where no island was,
a waste of sea transformed
into a world
that could be Paradise.
Grey through the mist
it sways and blurs

rocks, trees, and, nearer,
watchers
on the shingle
underneath the trees,
and then the black canoes,
strange words, strange cries,
the unexpected friendliness
of a dream
blessed with solidities
of rope and sail
and plank and creaking spar;
this is the moment
all of us remember
and can never
quite remember;
journal entries list
the gifts exchanged,
the costumes worn, the speeches
made with hands and gutturals,
and some names,
but they do not record
that sudden vision,
the gasp of miracle
and then its loss.
I drop the pebble
on the beach; there'll be
true splendour waiting
on a different shore.

II

Climbing up from the boat
rasped on the beach
and the heavy curve of the iron
locked on stones
into the forest,
alone in the brooding forest,
I watch in a patch of light
one thin leaf shaking
though all the leaves around it
were stiff and still,
one leaf at the very tip
of a tall plant shaking,
shaking helplessly, wildly,
as if caught
up in a private ecstasy
of music.
It stops as suddenly
as it began.

And I continue.
There are no more maps.
Can I expect a clearing,
a ruined well,
or just incessant forest?
Reindeer moss
beards overhanging boughs;
gold lichen eats
the sunlight on dead trunks;
grey lichen, stiff

as weathered lead,
snaps underneath my footstep,
and a chipmunk chatters
as a deer
leaps suddenly from brush.
I catch my breath
and think of landmarks
for my children's names.
From that knoll
there's a chance that, looking back,
I may see where I've come from

and recall
what set me climbing.
I cannot recall
more now than the impulse
to go on
however far to find
whatever place
it is that I must find,
a shaking leaf
possessed by solitary
passion, freed
(or trapped) by some
digression of the will

which, of a sudden, fails.
I stand stock-still,
confused, unable.
Wind moves through the leaves
and the whole earth has changed.

I've come too far.
Another step commits me
from my world
and to what otherness?
A rising panic
grits my teeth.
Deliberately, I turn.
There's nothing here.
And nothing comes of nothing

but perhaps the
nothingness. I face
the nothingness. My face
stares breathless back.

III

This is what we seek
who seek the sudden
leap of the heart at a
woman's turning head,
a marble fragment
of a god, a scrawled
and fading signature,
or else an island
where no island was,
a space of sea
transformed into a country
and a prayer

as this is now transformed;
grey through the rain
it sways and blurs
rocks, trees, and, nearer, watchers
on the shingle
underneath the trees,
and then the black canoes
like drifting trees
edging towards us,
and strange cries, strange words,
the unexpected friendliness
of a dream
thrust whole into the actual
life of breath
and rope and beam and sail.
This is the moment
of discovery
uncovering time
and this they tell of,
though they never tell
that this is also every
birth and death
transfiguring the dream
and the despair
with sudden shocking unity,
the cry
of life's astonishment
at being life,
the gift of the unknown
to the unknown,
as I continue.

There are no more maps.
Can I expect
log cabins in a clearing,
and a hermit, or a crone,
or perhaps
the remnants of a well
where gold was drowned,
or just incessant forest?
Reindeer moss
shags overhanging boughs;
gold lichen spreads
itself across dead logs;
grey lichen, stiff
as beaten lead, breaks
underneath my footsteps,
and a chipmunk chatters
in a rage:
clearly the inhabitants
have left,
if ever there were inhabitants.
I blaze
a wound upon a tree,
the axe-blow echoes
back from slopes and steeps
I cannot see.
Behind me I am sure
the boat is gone.

IV

I tell I myself that these
are the nineteen seventies,
and there are no mysteries left.
A deer
leaps suddenly from brush.
I catch my breath.
Another creature glimmers
on a stump
ten paces off and then
becomes no more
than uptorn root
and tangled leaf and briar.
I wipe away the sweat
and ease my pack.

I name the landmarks
with my children's names
as I encounter them
or see them distant.
Nicholas Rock is still
a half mile off
over the other side
of the swampy meadow;
Alison river, glistening, idling,
spreads
around it before gathering
somewhere — close
(for I can hear it)
to Saint Brigid's Falls.

Again I wade through tangle.
From that knoll
I should be able to look back and see
whatever ship it is
that I have left
and guess, perhaps,
the century and the cause
for which I clamber.
I cannot remember
more now than the impulse
to go on
however far, to find
what I must find.
Earth teems with musk;
I want to find a woman
wet as this wet-brown bark
whose coppery limbs
envelop me in her;
I want to fall
into the deeper sleep
that breeds the music
each leaf listens for;
I want, I want …
I call *haloooo, halooo,*
and time returns
as I must now return
clumsy and wearied to the shore;
my wife
has made a fire; the kids
are skipping stones
out over the bright water:
one does five.

These are the nineteen seventies.
No more mysteries.
Except the mystery of how I came
to move back in this way,
for what discovery?
And what repetition?
I repeat
myself, rephrase my phrasings,
am repeated.
Discoveries are recurrent,
happen, startle,
vanish as a sudden mist.
I pick
a pebble, clench it,
hold it in my hand.
It first is miracle
and then is stone.

V

Halooo   Halooo

Someone no longer there
torments me with the presence
of his shade.

Halooo   Halooo

My children do not hear.
They skip the stones.
One has made ten and leaps
with pure astonishment.

If I go down
they may prove old
as if I had returned
from centuries in the land of light
or slept
their lifetimes through.
                              I hesitate.
Beyond
their dancing shapes a ship
looms through the clear
eye-dazing blue as if
the blue were mist
and there are figures on the bows
stick-black,
and gesturing. I cannot hear.
My head
bends under weights of kingship
and I shake
to hear the gutturals
clumsy in my throat
and see from all the trees around
the tribe
assembling....
                    By the fire
my wife stirs logs.
The sparks fly up and scatter
out like stars
into our history.
Is this then our history?
Or every history
reaching out to bind

us all in moment upon moment,
moments
gathered piece by piece
from all the years
of tide that have surged back
and forth upon
this timeless beach
that shudders as I call

Halooo   Halooo

The children answer back.

Haloooo
        I pick a stone.
I drop a stone.
And am returned.
From what am I returned?

There in a patch of light
is one leaf shaking
though all the leaves around
are stiff and still,
caught up in private
ecstasies of music
none but it can hear.
I hear my heart
and see myself,
a ghost upon the sands
before the ever-moving waves,
and watch

my children running through me
as if mist
or a forgotten memory,
throwing stones
again into the huge
recurring sea
as if a stone could alter
all the flow
and shape an instant
to a monument
outlasting all that we
ourselves outlast
through episodes of every
life and death
our shifting stars command.
The leaf is stilled.
I walk down to the shore.
The fire burns.

III
MESSAGES FROM A
DIFFERENT MOUNTAIN

MESSAGES

1

Talk by a poet for poets.
Note one: don't talk.
Recite, or drink, or listen,
stood together
under an echoing tree.
Note two: Remember
someone is always climbing
a different mountain.

2

I look towards you now.
I have been looking
towards you all these years
but now, ashamed,
I let you behold the cataracts.
I can't see
anywhere but inside
the cavern of rock.

3

Wanton as autumn
I scatter these scribbling leaves
to bare the bough to the wind.
When all are gone
and the sap returned to the source
I shall not watch fires,
but, hid in the egg of the earth,
become my serpent.

4

We watch a hawk hunt shrike
across his garden,
the first hawk ever we saw here,
swerving, dipping
along from the plum to the lilac
and then back,
broad winged, questing, also
learning the silence.

5

I have spent a lifetime
studying Life.
This is supreme Narcissus,
the avid mirror.
In my deathtime
shall I study Death
or break the glass
and walk into the music?

6

After a time
what matters to us is not
the startling exactitude
of sudden wit,
but the nature of order:
waves return
endlessly, endlessly
from a blurred horizon.

7

Syllables all include
the shape of the teeth
and the beat of the breath on the
tongue, teeth, palate; all
include the shape of the jaw
and the shape of the skull
beating against the pressures of the sky.

8

Sacred, what else?
There are bulls, brutal
with torn grass, stamping;
there are gods
smaller than pebbles;
there are rivers
streaming like silk
from Her seated knees.

9

Salute the tiger in the
spoon. Attend the
snake's division of your
meat. Expose
the wolf paw in the cup.
Address your words
always to the blood upon the
door post.

10

The wastes between each
headless butte are travelled
still by wordless men
and lifeless horses;
we send messages
that rot in black
stained leather satchels
under altering trees.

11

Not poetry, not even verse,
but a kind of talking
that makes both poetry and verse
an affectation:
this is one description of
of achievement
The second is: What makes
talk sound like silence.

12

My beard has thickened
and suddenly I'm reminded
of the Good Samaritan
in a picture book
I got one birthday
and I bend, ashamed,
above that battered, crumpled,
plundered childhood.

13

Yesterday I remembered
again, and you,

cradling your head on my chest,
your relentless breathing

pulling you down into sleep,
again resisted

everything but our god
on the far far mountain.

14

We steer by negatives,
define the light
by contradiction,
mass most shadow where
illumination haunts:
it is the night
which answers us
with indecisive dreams.

15

The language of love is impossible
to a century

so completely obsessed
with the language of love.

I take my mirror
into the hall of mirrors

only because it cannot
contain your face.

16

I walk through the words of my words,
a corridor leading

its own career and existence,
past door on door

in an endless winding of wisdoms,
an echoing vision

deep in the heart of a mountain
where no one comes.

17

There is the night;
I see it over there.

When will I hold it within me
and see the day?

18

Should you wish to learn
the art of existence

which is the art of poetry,
do not fear
anything but the fear
of walking naked
into a forest filled
with the sound of buttons.

19

Where prophecy and fantasy intersect
the bird becomes the woman, the woman the bird;

where cloud and sun collide the light is splintered
into the lances of redeeming angels.

20

Ignore the audience?
Right!
          But in the way
the tree ignores the sky
as it lifts towards it
everything it can lift,
or the way the river
is careless about the rocks
that give it voices.

21

Partly it is a matter
of arranging
light so that it shows

a rainbow broken
up into the pattern
of the carpet
on which darkness
walks into the sun.

22

To moralize
is to despise the fact;

to live is to transform it
into music.

23

Authority negates
both will and instinct;
will and instinct
authorize form
not law.

24

If you believe I am a teacher,
teach me

the way to retain your ignorance
as the tree

retains the sweet of the earth
and shadows the earth

leaning into the springtime
like a fury.

25

I cannot recall
the cancelling of my beginning;

only slowly does the
cloth unfold

from the shining limbs of the goddess
and Her spasm

remains a star in the mind
till it eats the flesh.

26

Each poem, a scorpion
between stones,
black and pincering,
scuttles, halts,
lifts its great-jawed
lobstering rump,
awaits, inevitably,
Achilles.

27

Hours are too scant
for labour on trivial messages;

hours are too few for silence;
called to speak,
I must attempt the real:
outside my window
dandelions storm
into the sun.

28

Those who say Nonsense
of the words on the rock
have found the key to the lock
but not the door.
Those who say Truth
are standing before the door
but with no key to hand;
their worlds keep turning.

29

I will not deny that I have
too many friends.
I will accept all
save the black begrudgers.
Even these I will not
quite deny,
touching their padlocks
with these seas, these rivers.

30

It is important
always to hold

order and virtue
in different hands,

important always
to keep truth

and passion separate
until

the cadence unifies,
the calling

voice, dissolving,
becomes its message.

31

Do not wish for interpreters
with their wands
of white and black,
their syllables of air
trapped between lightnings;
only pray for lightnings
dazing the sudden landscape
into cadence.

32

I too am a student
I'm learning dying.

33

So much depends upon
a word that the word
begins to deny itself,
to claim clouds, trees,
rivers, mountains,
and the primal
shock of the sudden pulse
that dies at language.

34

There are an infinite number
of possible meetings;
this is one of the number,
and perhaps the least
significant and perhaps
the most. Who knows?
Ripples widen, widen
ripples on ripples.

35

Ultimately poetry
is unimportant.

Ultimately there is
only life
spilling into flower
above the coffin,

floating its bright seed far
on the breathless air.

36

I am expected to tell
the dangers of song

to children that think danger
is life or death

and have never slid their thumbs
on the edge of light

or known the eyes of a bird
destroy the mind.

37

When the window is entirely
covered in dust

what point is there in talk
of falling snow?

38

The darkness retains the darkness.
It is itself

its own gown and artificer.
It bends

only within itself,
kneels, mourns itself,

pierced by the random
innocence of stars.

39

A small poem for you
would be a poem

small as a snowflake
its crystal structure

spelling a single
speck of the blinding

mad white storm
or the eye of an angel.

40

Here I make love.
In this. In this.

What is sacrosanct
about flesh

that it alone can?
I make love

here, now, here …
The bride-songs rise.

41

If I attempt to describe
the way to poetry,
I do so because the route
is a crooked route
and wayward as the leap
of the heart is wayward,
leading as often towards
as away from silence.

42

Light spends time.
Look at the closest mirror,

see the shapes you were,
what you have died from.

43

Poetry does not matter.
I make poetry

as a stream shapes rocks.
It is the stream

that is the occasion
of the perfected stone;

only the stone, however,
may speak of water.

44

So you are all,
individually, right!

This I do not deny.
I do not deny,

either, the rightness of rock
in the running river,

the rightness of children
to gape at the falling sun.

45

I make with enormous care
an elaborate object.
Between my feet and yours
lies a green canal.
I throw the object into the
water, watching
ripples trouble you.
Me too they trouble.

IV
LOVE MAKING

THE GIFT

I would send you
a rose, golden
and flared wide,
but there's no rose
wide and golden
enough to spell
out the sunlight
that I would send.

I would send you
a prayer, but all
those words are wooden;
their hasps rust.
I would send you
a ring, but rings
are meant for lovers,
and we are less.

Therefore I send
not rose, prayer, ring
but this which brings
what I would send.

THE HEARING

(EnglynionY Clyweit)

Lover, have you learned to hear,
whispered in the secret ear,
Love is all that love should fear?

Have you heard the blackbird sing,
lifting up its burnished wing,
Love is darkness quarrelling?

Have you listened to the sound
of the night owl on its round,
Love is what the vole has found?

Have you heard at end of night
rafters creakingly recite,
Love is burdened by the light?

Have you woken to the spell
rising from the moss-coped well,
Love is Heaven kissing Hell?

Have you turned your head to hear
from the grasses on the weir,
Love is far, but Death is near?

Has the sudden trodden stone
greeted you with helpless moan,
Love must mourn and lie alone?

Have you heard the plover cry
from the ploughland to the sky,
Love is cloud run careless by?

Have you listened to the snail
chaining leaf with silver trail,
Love is beak and Love is nail?

Have you, tossing in your sheet,
heard the whisper at your feet,
Love is but a garnished meat?

Have you heard within the wave
rearing from the seaman's grave,
Love will drown what Love would save?

Yet, for all this, have you heard
with each dark and warning word,
Love is what God's finger stirred?

THE WOMAN

Flesh bulges as she drags her corset down,
unloosens brassiere; two swinging tits
nudge the slack belly; hair cascades her frown
and tired eyes; hands smooth the stiffening hips.

Clothes lie disordered on a chair; she bends
to straighten nylons; quagging buttocks shake;
blue veins behind the knees, marks of the brassiere
between the shoulderblades, lift love awake.

Ignorant of beauty, rueful and ashamed
of thick trunk, slack breasts, broad flank, at the glass
she stands on splayed feet, scratching; nervous tremors
ripple the vast abandons of her ass.

Turns to the bed then, reaching for a covering,
her belly wrinkling, unaware of eyes
that bless and reverence her tangled glory
black-bushed between the flaccid marbled thighs,

unaware that this used flesh she squanders,
bullies and hides, this signature of mass,
brings him within the darkness of earth's centre
the vast extremities of crotch and breast

more surely because creased, worn, tensed, and soiled,
it is all creatures' allegory — this
love's own close universe, all humankind
labouring within her hot involving kiss.

A CHAIN OF DAISIES

At thirteen older than I,
her small coughs gently
pecking at daisies,
she was colt-legged Deirdre
breathy with laughters
round the lawn. She died,
the daisy petals tipped, then
blotched with red.

I cough now, a smoker's
cough: blue air
sags with tobacco
smoke, my chest
tightened by memory;
my heart pounds,
carrying weights of
serious middle age
up stairs into their
sagging married bed.

Those whom the Gods love
hide. I seek
through empty gardens where
her laughters hopped
and coughed that idle
summertime. My wife
eases her corset down,
heavy for bed.

And I can't tell her
what I think. It seems
ridiculous: a thin

flat-chested girl,
grassblades sticking to my
knees, crouched there
upon the balding
lawn, her chains
of daisies lengthening through
my smaller hands.

It sounds ridiculous;
and she, too, clowned,
laughed till her breath
gave out, then sat
fanning her yellow head
with dockleaves, crinkling
nose and eye to
ridicule my doubt.

She was so wise, and
coughed so much. The bed
sweats years of weariness
and love. I turn
for reassurance. Heart
bumps as we come
together, breathless
almost as this girl
arranging daisies in
my mind. I sleep
heavily, as God sleeps
who dreams us all.

A LEAF OF PRIVET

If this leaf
means anything
it does not
mean as words do.
You agree to that?

If these words
mean anything
they do not
mean as kisses do.
Is that agreed?

Now you expect
a third term
in progression.

I will not provide it.
I will say

only that your mouth,
shaped like a leaf,
engrosses me
with its half–
troubled smile.

PALIMPSEST

It is to be in love with a woman
long held by another man,

her voice, her turning head, her hands'
unthinking gestures, part of him.

It is to know that there are moments
when she smiles that you become

almost the kindred of that man.
It is to know these moments few.

It is to be without the words,
the inner knowledge of the words,

her heart's familiars, moving through
her days of comfort and despair

with an assurance you have lost.
It is to think her memory on

another place, another woman,
footprints bruised into the stone.

THE RESOLUTION

Though writhing nightly
in my bed, protesting
desperate love, she still
repeats her firm
resolve to end it
from the highest motives,
always from the very
highest motives,
truth, integrity,
her absent husband,
and her shame, her planned
assenting shame.

BY THE LAKE

Under our window
we may see
a beach, a boat,
a twisted tree,

and, far across
the shining lake,
a mountain changing
green to black

as wind scuds cloud
in from the West
and shakes the tree
to an unrest

that ripples water,
rocks the boat,
and sends the fingers
to your throat

in sudden fear
that this might be
the start of dark
for you and me.

SUPPOSE

Suppose the moon,
and then suppose
beside the restless
hushing sea
our silence as
we pace the sand,
hand sharing hand;
suppose that we,

lost to all other
earth, confess
our secret solitudes,
expose
the nakedness
we bring to love,
the simple happiness;
suppose

that one of us
should then foresee
and fear the world's
censorious look —
then would the moon
and tide and sand
draw back and leave
but barren rock.

EROSION

The cliff crumbles;
the clay slides
down; my arm
around your waist,

I watch a brown sea.
Foam on foam
piles, ripples
a sour yeast

far beneath us;
the wind's whip
lashes the hair
across your eyes

red-brown as clay:
Hold tight! Hold tight!
Or there's no shoring
in our lies.

NIGHT POEM, VANCOUVER ISLAND

I

The wind's in the west tonight,
heavy with tidal sound;
the hush and rattle of trees,
the indrawn breath of the shore,
do what they must; waves slap
at the tip and stagger of stones,
and the night tonight is black;
blackness without intent
moves over the globe
as waters move. The shoals
are nosing into the storm.

Blackness moves over the globe.
Will this wind never drop?
The house, awash with air,
swings into the dark,
and, all its lamps ablaze,
challenges time and fear.
I see a wall of ice.
Newspapers fall like flowers.

Turn in the bed, my Love.
Reach out. We almost touch
but, swimmers pulled apart
by arbitrary tides,
are swept out on the night.
Somewhere a hand will find
that delicacy of bone
locked in a glacial year.

We label history now.
Fossils, our smiles extend
the frontiers of the past.
Our kisses breed new terms.

The sea speaks as it must.
We lie together in
a hollow of the sound,
clasped hands entangling bones.
We have our prayers to say.
We have our seed to spend.
We half believe in day.

Sleep is difficult now.
Loudly the pump of the heart
and the rasp of sheet on sheet
answer voice with voice.
Turn in the bed, my Love.
We were a distant tribe
that died. These waters move
the history from our bones.

II

Darkness begins and ends
all that we have and are;
stilled in this night of gale
on the long death of a bed
I reconstruct such lives.
I hear the forest birds
scream over the shore.

I watch the slide of light.
Does history begin?
Feet beat upon bare earth.
Whales rise in the sea.

Something created here:
logic travelled moss
upon the hospitable boles
and lichen dribbled song
from boughs the bines make laws.
Walking to rules of boughs,
listening to wings in the pulse
and breakers over the heart,
I become stone. I pause
to accept the tread of the sun
and the worm under my cold.
Clay is part of me. Grass
patterns me; meshed in rain
by grass, I stare like a toad.
Prayers rot on me like fern.

Do not touch me. Look,
but do not touch. My smile
has red meat in its teeth.
My skin is soft with fur,
and I am wiser than dogs.
Your mouth upon my mouth,
your freed persuasive breasts
could end a different tale
but are irrelevant here.
Press close. Your V of hairs

and buttery mandible nip
most freedoms in the bud,
and your haunches ride
the nightmare to its knees,
but I am not the night,
or free, or beast, or king.
I have no dark or bed.

  Light slid up to the shore
here from the stiff sea.
Trees were huge with rain
and the square teeth of bears.
Eagles reach their wings
out above whales; head down,
a toad stood on the lip
of speech and sang its flies.

  I am afraid. The hunter
only obeys the laws
of chastity and death.
I do not know his code
that changes as herds grow
or lessen, hungers change.
The salmon leap up through
the membrane. Narrowing hills
shudder, contract, and rip
all they can get. The gun
is levelled, the bow drawn.
Time has its lives to eat.

III

Abandon me. I am lost
in the sweat of my own dark.
Rivers include my eyes.
Forests evolve my hands.
Over the valley hawks
gather into the eye,
watching the movements of death.
I am a name for the sea.

Leave me. Let me be.
Somewhere the ships turn home,
the animals bless the sun,
the thundering lungs fall still,
and the stone eyes smile.
Something created me
because of that one place.
I wear it round my bones.

Who is a wooden mask
painted with teeth. I stood
alone on the island for days
until a whale spoke out.
Its eye was a bead of blood,
its fin curved as an adze,
and its head a hill.
Who is an ivory jaw,
a black glistening skin,
a boat floating alone.

How is a scar on a rib.
I have forgotten craft
and practice. Knives obey
orders I cannot give,
having no rules or words.
Fish come to my hand.
How is a crooked bone,
a bird dropped on the wing.

Why is not my business.
Causes are different worlds.

IV

I am the sound you make.
Leaf, twig and stone
compose me like a song.
I am the inch you crawl
closer, lifting the bow.
I am the lens of air
through which the hunted move.
We are creation's kind.
Look out! An eagle falls
in every seed we spit.
Fish jump in every thumb.
We are destruction's kin.
Be still. A heron soars
in each astonished breath.

V

Something created here
the lives time has to eat.
Something invented time,
a wrinkle upon the sea.

Only the dead awake.
The living have no need.
Lapped in a fold of water
travelled across the glove
to end up finally here,
I lift up my arms,
but not to Death. I kneel
but not to Love. I hold
existence close, not beast,
or god, or man, but breath,
more simple and less sure.

Come now, if you wish.
The wind from the west has stilled.
Your mouth upon my mouth
solves nothing but is good.
Light rises from the sea
and time spreads with the light.
Put your body to mine;
we are the world we caused.

DON'T GET ME WRONG

I didn't mention it
in the other poem,
(which isn't printed here),
because I'd hate
for you to think I like
your lovely body,
(which I do)
more than your haunting verse,

for I do not (I mean,
prefer your body).
Nevertheless I'd like
to mention that
your loving is as
memorable as your lines,
in case you think
by leaving that theme out

I meant to hint that I
delighted in
your verse more than your bed,
(which I do not),
though verse lasts longer
in a way. I don't
mean you are getting old
or losing shape;

I simply mean the poems
stay on the page
and do not change,
whereas you leave your bed,

remake your face,
transform yourself. I did
not care to mention it
in the other poem

because it could be
misinterpreted,
and poets are good at
misinterpretation;
it's our profession,
as, of course, is love,
which you well know
so I've not mentioned it.

V
CLOSER NOW
For Her

THE SEPARATION

Since it becomes us
to keep this
exact and difficult
space between us

for reasons given
and other reasons,
(so must the heart,
in trouble, hide),

I send you words
to make this space
itself a quality
of affection,

sharing with you
this distance that
enables messages
to be heard.

OVERTURE

Listen. This is
desperate. Listen.
I am the nervous
start in the dark
before sleeping,
the knee jerking,
the twitch of the lip
at a dreamed kiss,

and hide in your finger
as you touch
her breast or pick
the brush, the pen,
the razor turning
your wet cheek
and straining throat
to the lick of time.

I am confession,
the itch, the tic,
the morning erection,
the slow qualm
filling the belly,
the knees' tremble,
everything unintended,
known

only slowly
and known hidden,
the bones in the closet,
the lost names,

the dangerous memories,
the outrage
hidden and laughing
behind the house.

Shall I tell you
I am a liar?
You know that.
You know, too,
my lies are your lies,
your discoveries.
Have you remembered
that girl's name —

the one with the little
breasts that sat
across you, giggling?
Do you recall
the smell of her armpit,
her bad tooth?
Listen to this disc —
they were "records"

then when you heard it
first. Do you
remember the sea-sick
lurch of the gut
at such beauty,
the sweet sadness,
calling that vomit
"our tune"?

Do you? Do you?
I remember
everything now.
The bones upstand.
Does it matter
if mine or yours?
Names are the first
things we pretend,

but not the most
important. Listen.
This is desperate.
I am trapped
in memory's riot,
carried through
everything that
bones lay claim to.

EVERYTHING

Everything is in the light of everything, holy.
But do not expect a catalogue of grace,
trees, leaves, grass, and children suddenly shouting
Hi-Hi, loudly, running in their playground,
for to select is always to leave out something
quiet, unnoticed, like the snail shell lying
under the black and rotten bit of the gatepost,
or the swing of the signature on the paper,
all of a movement. Everything is moving
in its own direction, sure as owls
dipping the blind hedges, the small stone walls,
in the stiff hills where everything keeps house
within the sound of wind, each, any stirring
slowly towards itself, defeat and conquest,
end and beginning meaningless, arrival
only a word to stand for somewhere else
imbued with what we are more than ourselves.
And this we must remember: every thing
is, before everything, holy and astir
with an unfolding plenitude we are
the heirs of and bequeathers to our sons.
Therefore be thankful when you thank; be sure
when time assures you on the dragging path;
be kind when you are kindred; do not lend
uncertainties to strangers or take truth
away from anyone, but still be still
in movement and in peace, the language turning
always upon your silence. Look around.
Everything, before everything, is yours
and none an island — no, none, none, not one
but is the others'. We possess ourselves

only so far as others lean to us
and draw us, moving, into their stirred house
as easily as air, only so far
as everything remains itself and sings.

OPENINGS

Openings:
The ice widens
darkness between blind mirrors
where I walked that winter, sliding
seven years of breathless life
between hedges;
ice widens
darkness between the crags of light
and mounded whiteness of a North
I must imagine if I dare
to speak of winter, dare to think
of openings in the frozen mind
that must break open into darkness,
opening in the darkness forms
of goat, of bear, of swan, of cross,
of mathematics of the light
that calculate the track of time
and openings in time.
I see
time opening and retreat, recall
there was an opening in the cloud
that showed a sudden country, green
and definite where purple sea
spread wide its cloak till then, a place
unmapped, ephemeral. Clouds closed
and engines rumbled.
We are over
land. This is your Captain speaking.
The local time is now high noon
and elsewhere midnight.

She at midnight,
opening her gifts, it is
my birthday now, so can I open?
You may open. It's a love!
Truly a love! How did you find it?
opening wide her tired eyes
as if through black and narrow rocks
green-stained by tide and scarred by tide,
holding her breath, expectant, she
had happened on another sea
of limitless irradiance with
a smooth expanse of untrod sand
that only children trust and know
belonging upon every shore
of every proper ocean and
no place for ice.
Ice opens, dark
the widening water, dark the night,
and dark the mirror, bright the stars
through whose far mesh we seek to move
to farther openings.
We call
them "openings", those gaps that we
must push through in our affluent dream
of progress gathering age and praise
until we face an opening that
we can't avoid but stumble through,
helpless, never having paid
attention to that hidden fault
hair-triggered to bring ruin down,
replace a mountain with a sea,

the lakes with deserts, deserts with
the slow inevitable forests

to be named by others who
are still to come, or who have gone,
for this is not of Earth but Time
and it is Time that is the fault
which opens suddenly into
another opening
and another opening.

MAKING A POEM FOR CHRISTMAS

Make me a poem for Christmas?
I make a poem

with lambs, a crib, some
shepherds and a child

that doesn't cry but
nestles in harsh straw

as if he were in bliss —
I'd say he was

at least six months;
somehow he won't come out

as crumpled pink and
dribbling as he should,

and she, the mother, is all
dressed in blue

and has a dazed expression.
I am dazed

myself and make another poem.
The poem

has three old men, two white,
one black, in robes,

each carrying a
jewel-encrusted box,

kneeling around a cradle,
and the child

now, surely, twelve months old,
is smiling, sweet,

both blue eyes focussed
perfectly, hair blonde.

It's no good. Everything
gets in the way;

the myths, the legends
carols, hymns, and prayers

roar louder than the
loudest army chorus

parading Disney figures
on the screen.

Surely there must be
another way:

poor people huddled from
the dreadful weather

in a stable smelling of
stale urine

cow-breath plumes upon
the frost-filled air,

and the baby swaddled up
so tight

only a small button nose
is showing,

and the mother
anxious and exhausted

lying back on straw,
her husband pacing

up and down, flapping
his arms and saying

"Maybe tomorrow you'll
be strong enough

and we can go on
and get out of this,"

she nodding wanly,
then the baby crying,

confused and fretful.
But you don't want that —

you want a celebration
and a paean

of praise, an organ tone
of moving sound,

or maybe crystal
tintinabulations,

flashing lights.
kaleidoscoping joy

upon the decked and laden tree,
and crackers

tugged, bang, with their
riddles and their mottoes,

and the turkey crisped
bright bronze and slicing

cleanly, with the sausages,
brussel sprouts,

baked potatoes, gravy,
then the lying

back in armchairs groaning
gently, stirring

now and then to eye
the fuzzy screen

and Tiny Tim godblessing us....
It's still wrong.

If I must make a
Christmas poem I must

make it much shorter
and say only:
        This

midwinter in the dark
time of the year,

give, and be thankful;
fill the house with light

to bring the light,
to bring the love, the peace

the story holds up to us
like a dream

from which we must not
ever fully wake

if years are to continue
on this earth.

NAMES

Do not use too many names,
for names

are separations,
and we all are one

in past and present;
names reverberate

particulars till the
unity is drowned

in vast obliquities
of sound and image;

rather speak of
Her without a name,

of Him without a name,
retaining thus

the rhythm of the breath:
Her Him, Her Him,

Her Him, Her Him, Her Him,
our endless music.

WOODTOWN MANOR, DUBLIN
for Garech de Brun

The peacock cries.
I tug nettles
free of the black earth,
haul the rose
clear of encumbrance.
The stone house
shimmers in sunlight.
The road swerves

through muddled meadows
to far mist
dwindling the city.
I retreat,
straighten my back,
my hands cut,
stung, bitten,
my shirt wet,

black with the sweat
of more years
than years can number.
The peacock cries
again, again;
the rank grass
drags at the thousand
trailing eyes

as earth has always
dragged. Heat
drums in my skull.

I gasp, glut
on the cold wine.
The bird's cry,
full-throated,
tears the heart,

rips at the stones,
the cry of pride
alone with history.
I bend
again to the tangle
of the green,
wrenching with ancient
useless hands.

QUATERNION

I

Seeing Her in Her various disguises,
broad wife, black-sheathed schoolgirl, swinging tart,
blonde, brown, lissom, squabby, moist-eyed, dozy,
how can he tell realities apart
enough to know which one will fit his crown
and drag across the stage Her blinding curtain?
Only the unsought, unthought, strange-eyed bitch
will plague that itch and make his verses certain.

II

Offend Her, if you must, with random women,
drink, drugs, thievery, or lay nations waste —
these She may tolerate as venial, but
once boast of cunning or inflate your taste
into a principle of separate rule,
you'll feel the downturn of that sovereign hand,
and, old or young, cold scholar or hot fool,
will tumble, gaunt and wordy, with the damned.

III

This man who is dead made poems.
                                        .   Now on his grave
I scatter public leaves, gloss-darkened holly,
spotted laurel, blue-green ferns of yew,
woven into a hubless, spokeless, holy
wheel — the usual dismissive token
of the turning year, and of completion.

But the Angel sorrowing above stone
in stone humility his heirs provide
I give no leaf to; she leans, gravely dressed
in robes and misery, who should bestride
this huddle, arms akimbo, out-thrust hips,
bared breasts, wild hair, triumphant parted lips.

IV

Wrestle this Angel, and whoever falls
to head-lock, arm-lock, hip-tilt, threshing thigh,
it is Her victory, or none at all.

Hers is that last, wild, conquering, plundered cry.

YOUR MISTAKE

In a bright blue skirt and a red blouse
she is making pastry,

rolling it out on the board,
the small hairs glistening

on her forearms, her buttocks
clenched and sturdy,

her feet a little apart.
She is not my wife.

My wife is someone else.
She brushes back

a tendril of light blond hair
and sprinkles flour

on the pale brown board,
(she is not my daughter),

her full breasts rising and falling;
She is humming

softly under her breath.
She is not my lover.

THE BALL
for Michael Seward Snow

Under the rock is an iron ball.
If you lie on your belly you'll see it there,
jammed between rock and rock at the top
of the roofed-in creek, so changed by air
and sea and age that its orange rust
burns like a sun. It is held fast where
rock roof meets rock. If you slither down
on a rope, he said, you can get quite near.

If you once get down, avoiding the pool
that is three foot deep, worn round by a stone
turning and turning upon the spool
of the spinning tide, and are big enough fool
to wedge your shoulders into that gap
you can touch the ball. It is rough with rust
and orange and ochre and red, he said,
a sun clamped down by a granite crust,

but you'll never move it. The sea is loud
as your heart as you lie on the slime and shift
your hand past your head as you chin the stone,
and every time that you try to lift
a muscle or twist the tide seems near
and the rock roof closer. The ball burns red
where roof meets rock: I hid it there
when I was a child of God, he said.

ROBERT GRAVES IN DEYA, MALLORCA

A single rock,
the pierced ear of the sea,
below the Deya road,
and by the road
the village guardian,
a lone stone pine
overlooking hills
of terraced rock,
establish ambience.
In any place
a hundred poems have spoken
there is this
assertion by the landscape:
it may be
in crag, or lake, or cave,
or broken tower
fanged against sunset
or a flight of swans
blessing the still lake water
under trees,
but always in that place
earth frees its themes.
There dreams evolve through earth
and earth through dreams
till every image
is of both and one
with every happening
of speech and stone.

So Deya is, because of him.
He comes
down to the terrace,

underneath his arm
a basket of black olives,
on his head
the straw hat of a peasant
from the fields,
a strong, worn, honoured man
admiring earth.

Lemons and oranges
flare within the green
below the terrace edge
and sapling beech
(boca and book)
are offerings at his door.

Poetry is studying
how the spirit soars
on learned as on simple
ignorant things.
An inch-long Pegasus,
its green-bronze wings
arrogant, fragile,
stands upon a sill.
The stone house throbs and
echoes like a bell.

Events are of belief
and not of act.
All history is credence,
and all truth
the image of an ambience

that exacts
the proper tribute
from the humbled mind.
So Poetry knows,
knows more the less it proves.
Explain? said Goethe,
I will not explain
anything I have written.
Vision lives
that one dimension
closer to the sun
than all we measure by,
and Time, absurd,
becomes a mesh of shadows
cast by that
entrancing light poets enter
to meet Death
in every poem they make
and be reborn
by virtue of the poem
which alters earth
around them.

      Thus in Deya,
as we talk,
the sapling beeches
reach up to the sun
the natural language
of the timeless Muse
who is the Light that casts
these shadows, words.

Conclusions are not.
Everything attends
the every scene and minute.
Though we part,
a hand stays on a book,
a basket set
upon a wall holds olives
black with light
and oranges burn, picked,
upon the trees
that are both seed and kindling,
fruit and flame.
What matters is not scholarship
or fame
but being both of shadow
and of light,
of root and air,
of furnace and of sea,
of Time and of
eliminated Time.

We drive from Deya,
bearing Deya home.

VI
LETTERS TO THE DEAD

WOOD

for Naoko Matsubara

There is nothing that cannot be
wood-spoken,

lettered in wood
and spelled out strong by wood,

the language knurled and gnarled
by years of trees,

the syllables a sway
of leaves and boughs,

the thought a dark thought
dipping through the root

to chills of water
hidden deep within

the fundamen, the dream
a shining dream

shaking its leaf to sky
and sky on sky.

There is nothing that cannot
be wood music,

nothing, nothing, nothing;
smoothed and carved

and blessed and healed,
wood builds us, holds us, names us,

guards us, keeps us,
leads us through the doors.

BEGGING THE DIALECT
for Christopher Hanson

The crumpled villages, guide-booked and mapped,
of a flat land by a flat sea, cold and wet,
make my destination, caul in hand,
begging from door to door the dialect.

What is that? And that? And that? What did
your father call it? What his father? What?
The thin quick ribboning of the sentences
whirrs to record the pause, the slur, the act.

Broken and blurred, pitched out of the one key
to turn the wards round and unlock a place,
I play it back. You notice, if you look,
the old men all have the one watching face,

hardened like cart-ruts in a hard frost, made
all the same ridge and hollow. Playing back,
the lid reflects my darkly bended head
growing towards that sealed familiar mask
till I am asked, perhaps by my sons, *What*
do you call that? call that? The spool runs out.
Back again, I haunt them, caul in hand,
begging from door to door the dialect.

A BALLAD OF BILLY BARKER

A gay young widow woman
with eyes as green as glass,
and a bandy-legged prospector
with slum upon his ass;
you split your sides to think of it,
but I lie stiff as stone:
it's curtains now for English Bill
in Victoria Old Men's Home.

On Williams Creek in August
back in sixty-two
the claims ran dry. The black sand let
no speck of colour through.
Ned Stout came down the canyon
and found his gulch and struck;
I followed him, staked out my claim,
and drove down through the rock.

Jumped ship, I did, and followed up
the blinding yellow dream.
The Fraser lashed its rolling stones
till mud was silver cream;
the walls of Hell's Gate cliffed me in
and Jackass Mountain shook
its dirt-brown back in mockery as
I trailed to stake my luck.

Seven of us worked that shaft.
The sun danced with the heat.
Ten feet we went and nothing showed.
Ten feet and then ten feet.
At thirty feet the cloud came up;

the sky was solid lead;
the windlass juddered at each hoist;
the wind sobbed for the dead.

Seven of us choked for breath.
I went down in the pit
At forty feet the rain came down;
we took another foot.
A crazy sailor and six men
hauled rope till they were blind;
at fifty feet no colours showed
and even hope was mined.

Hope, Faith, Prayer were all mined out
and rubble piled up high
around the shaft-house hacked out from
the pines that hacked the sky;
mud welled; rain swaled; ropes cut and slid,
and heart and mouth were dry.

At sea the waters curve away
green satin from the bow,
and foam as thick as milk swirls out
along the track we plough,
and waves heave tall as hills and fall
like hills upon the deck.
The hills that stood round Williams Creek
would neither bend nor break.

The hills that frowned their forest black
above our hunch and sweat
rocked no horizons for our eyes,

nor shone out in the night
with greens and blues and grains of gold
as I've seen on the sea.
We took another foot. The dream
stood shuddering over me;

the yellow dream, the blinding dream
I'd taken for my life
stood over me. I felt its breath.
Its eyes cut like a knife.
I took another foot. Time stopped.
I heard it end my life.

I heard it finish, and I struck.
Five dollars to the pan;
and seven men on Williams Creek
went crazy to a man.
A thousand dollars every foot
we took out from that clay
and seven men on Williams Creek
were blinded by the day.

Drinks we had. Three days we drank
and all on English Bill.
I think I drank a thousand lives
at every swig and spill,
a thousand miners trailing north,
a thousand narrow pits
upon the benches by the creeks
where golden bones would sit.

I think in every glass I saw
a face and then a face;

a woman with long yellow hair
leaned into my embrace,
a widow with eyes green as grass
and lips as red as blood,
but at her back another face
as black as the wet wood,

another face as black as wood,
with skin as soft as slum
and eyes as blind as pebbled quartz,
and gaping mouth as dumb
as Blessing's mouth, or Barry's mouth
that opened as he swung.

I met her in Victoria by
the bitter chilling strait.
Some traded skins. I traded gold
and traded for a mate,
a London widow woman
and her golden hair and luck:
I took her up the Fraser
through the roaring mocking rock.

I took her up to Barkerville;
I should have let her be.
The gold ran out; the claim ran dry;
she ran loose as the sea;
her greens of satin, foams of silk
heaved up to prow on prow:
the sea's a wicked smother, but
I know a worse one now.

The sea's a wicked country;
its green hills lift and drown:
but earth's a played-out working
when you've thrown your money down.
I worked as cook; I begged; I washed;
my pans were grey with stone:
it's curtains now for English Bill
in Victoria Old Men's Home.

It's headstones now for English Bill.
My drinking roaring mouth
bums cancer where her kisses burned
and has a graver drouth,
and as I gape I see her face,
but then that other face
that looked on me in Williams Creek
and rotted like the race —

the race of men that dragged their packs
up canyons to the creek,
the race that heard my pick crack down
into that yellow strike,
whose deaths built law and church and state
upon my broken stone,
but Billy Barker's dead and gone
in Victoria Old Men's Home.

ON THE EVE OF ALL HALLOWS

Histories walk tonight;
clad in accomplished fate,
each takes his grievous turn;
candles in turnips burn
their spearblades on the dark
and quiver in the talk,
the after-silence. Here,
at the old end of the year,
I was born. My star
rose in this watchful mirror.

Now quiet is possessed
by necessary ghosts;
they too, born in between
the tide and the tugging moon,
found violence in the nerve,
had pity, suffered love,
and ached at beauty. Death
sighs on our common breath
and mirror. Ghosts, stand by
this poet of your family.

Poetry has been my line
from snivelling childhood on;
I have the usual scars,
the usual haunted face,
am lecherous enough;
I even have a cough,
though so far don't spit blood;
I plague my wife: it's said
Art is the one thing for
which everyone must suffer.

I stare down at the glass;
behind me my own face
encounters me; I turn
and parings twist my name;
my own words fill my ears.
What will survive? The stars
may tell in time, at least
will sieve away the worst,
and probe with practised hand
the desolate remainder.

It is one thing to build
a poem and fix the world
around it, make it spin,
another to give stone
the lasting, bitten word.
Ghosts, listen. You have had
mortality's one proof;
I ask you for relief:
tell me these passions are
in more than the mind's mirror.

Some say poems have kept
a thought from being trapped
by staying on the move
like most wise beasts we have,
and some think them a mode
of clambering inside
the space between the fear
and the resultant prayer
of every man that wants
to last out the long moment.

I'd say mine were the lies
I had to fix in place
to keep Truth on the run,
for when the hunt is done,
the quarry faced, who knows,
as blood streams in the eyes,
what fingers grip? My hands
for purely mortal ends
tic knots which they untie
with difficulty, intently.

Nothing in me is fixed,
and nothing I have asked
comes from a firm desire;
I have no final prayer
tonight as my words all
turn ghosts within the still
and reckoning hour I face;
I claim no special grace,
for all my deaths are on
the point of being human.

I keep the mirror clean;
I watch it change, alone
with love of every nerve
of living that we have,
and see time unpick time.
I do not wear a name
except the end of speech.
The stars rock. And I reach
up from the drowning glass
my small necessities.

TO NORMAN NICHOLSON

What do the dead remember?
We'll not know
until we too are dead
and then can't tell
except through mediums
and table-tappings
which never do amount
to very much.
But I've a theory
that when I'm dead
I'll reach back sometimes
to those little things
that, like a pebble in a
pool, spread out
such widening circles
that I could not help
but touch infinities;
of course, they dwindled
into stillness
as do we all, and yet
remain a part of me.
And now I wonder
if you recall that
summer afternoon,
french windows open
on our tiny garden,
and sitting there recording,
just for us,
Rising Five and *Cleaton Moor*
and, most
entrancing of them all,

A Turn for the Better
which still haunts me,
though it's not the poems
alone but birdsong
coming in to join them
with another melody
so your words
were Orpheus bringing
music from the trees,
creation dancing
in the light of sound,
earth moving under us
as if it breathed,
sky quivering. And as your
husky, breathless
gentle syllables
became the swirled
and shaking blossoms of
perpetual summer,
the turbulence and the
shimmer of the rivers,
(your own Duddon one of them)
I caught
my breath as if I'd
snagged my sleeve upon
a twig of that all-spreading
tree which rose
that instant in our small
suburban garden
but had to drag it free
as we returned

together from somewhere
that may be where
you speak from now,
for I can hear you speak
not words but wisdoms
to me here, and send
this letter, sensing that
you do remember.

LETTER TO NICHOLAS
(1957–1994)

I have to talk to you.

                           Whatever I say
does not matter. It is not words that matter
but the need to speak, and I am speaking
to you now. I am saying what I am saying
because I am here and you are in an elsewhere
I cannot understand,

                        though you are smiling —
I sense that — and wish that I were smiling
with this sad white emptiness in my gut.

When you think of children it gets elaborate:
the gains and losses of words, the scrubbed raw knees,
the falls and furies, wool and serge and cotton,
laces, buttons, velcro.

                         When you think
of children it is impossible; they don't
belong where we belong, or if we do
belong at all they have belonging elsewhere
and it frightens.

                       I recall your childhood,
watching you watching, see you seeing, know
in twenty years or so we may meet somewhere
sometime, or may not.

                    This verse for you
comes from an old man blinking at the stars.

We have had some practice at separate lives;
now, however, we must learn again
the intimacy of long distance, the sharing of space,
the knowledge that no knowledge can ever be sure
as well as images — the hand, the smile,

the elbow on the table, the lifted glass —
but pictures are not persons, and persons are
not us at all when we meet, as we do,
between the minutes, where the minutes break
apart into their multitudes of stars.

No more now. Which might mean now is done,
but I don't quite mean that. I only mean
a pause in time within the clutch of time
and love to you, my son, love upon love.

FOR WILLIAM STAFFORD

i

I didn't know when you went,
hadn't known you were going.
Your voice is part of me still,
and your involution,
the way you talked until
a poem was happening
and the way that poem
slid back to earth,
and, oh, the eyebrows lifted
at succinct moments.
We met rarely
and were never close,
but how close, ever,
are those friends who share,
without thinking or telling,
a quiet conviction
and wear it in different weathers
by different hills?

ii

Bill, I am using you to make a poem.
You know this, of course, because you know
far better than most of us how the door swings open.
I remember watching you enter a party,
sidling hesitantly round the room
with a kind of modesty not disguising
a steady intention, a certainty, and a pride,
moving the way an antler moves through the forest,
inheriting and giving;

                             that is all,
perhaps, that we can manage: to inherit,
and to give, and sidle round the room.

iii

Somewhere you said that stumbling
always leads home.
I wonder whether my difficult
knees are relevant
to my seeking out
the room I need,
but I suspect you were in metaphor,
that overcoat we wear
against the wind.

But stumbling … yes,
you had the truth of it;
marching gets us nowhere,
that's for sure,
and we all stumble most
when we are learning
life from the beginning,
or, I guess,
when aging knees are difficult.
Right now,
I am stumbling
and am nearing home.

DEATH

in memoriam Dick Morriss

Death is not a happening
but a presence

as the builders
of the churches knew

and the makers of the
tombs, the painters

having him move long-legged
with his scythe

through the quivery grass
or seeing him

pallid in the shadows
at the ball.

Of course death is not always
gap-jawed, bony;

sometimes the form's a woman's,
her pale beauty

and low voice caressing
time to sleep,

sometimes a mist
that moves in from the sea,

sometimes a cry,
a night-borne lonely cry

even, some have said,
a creaking gate.

I think myself
death is an ampersand

linking this word, that word,
beyond the silence.

CLARE ABBEY

"Remember me when I am dead
and simplify me when I'm dead."
                              — Keith Douglas

Item, skull. A clutter of dry bones.
Several snapped and broken. At least one gnawed.
The Abbey window has no glass, the nave
is grass; the tombs are black holes fringed with nettles.
Wire prevents the sheep, at least; the tourists
hold their cameras clumsily at bad angles.

Simplify me. This is much too tangled
up with roots and gullshit.
Gulls come in
across the cliffs when winds blow up, and spit
white on the sepulchres, arraign the tower
in harsh voices.
Still, there are no snakes
since Patrick sent them packing,
and no rats.

What I was is nothing to you now
and could make memory difficult. I'd say
an easy lie is best.
Call me a poet.
That's an approximation few will care
enough about to doubt
or look me up
along the dark stacked corridors.
Explain
my life as dates
(Born Then, Died Then tells all)

and close this damned great gap:
I look so small
and complicated fools might think to search
for evidence of love affairs, or pride,
or sudden dangerous solitudes, and learn
more of me than I know.
I do not know
what happened or what mattered.
Keep me dead
and unacknowledged; I ask nothing more.
Simplify me. Then at last my name
will be the thing I was,
a moment's noise
you have no need to dignify or share.

24.III.88

i

This is a time
when the cat walks through the mirror
and all the mistletoe berries
fall like snow.

This is a time when the
red wine turns to silver
and the pillars of.the house are black.

This is the time
when, opening the cupboards,
we discover only crawling children.

ii

I have put out the light. The room is quiet.
Only the rustle of bedclothes shakes the air,

and yet a buzzing sound is nearing, circling,
nearer near, ceases, then begins

once more, and "There's a fly," you say, "a fly,
and I can't sleep." So I turn on the light.

There is no fly. No sound. No room;
no bed; no house; no life, no death.

Only the light.
And I put out the light.

ABOUT
ROBIN SKELTON

Robin Skelton was born in a schoolhouse in Easington, East Yorkshire, on October 12, 1925, with one broken thigh. The son of Cyril Skelton, the local schoolmaster, and his wife, Lili, he served as a signals clerk in the Royal Air Force in India from 1943 to 1947, after which he studied English literature at Leeds University. After graduating in 1951, he went on to lecture in English at the University of Manchester before leaving in 1963 for Victoria, British Columbia, to take a position at the newly opened University of Victoria.

Skelton arrived in Canada with a solid reputation in the United Kingdom and Ireland: as a poet, with three well-received collections; as a scholar of the Irish Renaissance, especially of John Millington Synge; as a champion of contemporary Irish poetry; and as the co-founder of the Peterloo Group of Poets and Artists and the Manchester Institute of Contemporary Arts. He had also worked extensively as a British Broadcasting Corporation arts interviewer, an experience that served him well when in 1967, along with John Peter, he founded *The Malahat Review*, which he edited until 1983, establishing it as one of the top English-language literary journals in the world. Under the auspices of *The Malahat Review*, he collected contributions from the leading writers of the age. In 1973 he made a pilgrimage to Mallorca to visit Robert Graves and, in the company of Peter

Russell, to Venice to visit Ezra Pound, an experience that led to his greatest single collection of poetry, *Timelight* (1974).

During his early years in Victoria, Skelton also worked extensively on a theory of scholarship that elucidated the creative practice of poets, which led eventually to his triptych of books on craft, *The Practice of Poetry* (1971), *The Poet's Calling* (1975), and *Poetic Truth* (1978), as well as to the creation of the University of Victoria Department of Creative Writing in 1973, where he taught until he retired in 1992. In the 1960s, Skelton also maintained strong contacts with the American writing community and could often be found in Seattle, where he helped promote the careers of both Richard Hugo and David Wagoner with his anthology *Six Poets of the Pacific Northwest*. For years he spent weeks every summer with Surrealist poets and painters in California in the company of his lifelong friend, the Victoria painter Herbert Siebner. Out of this experience came his books of "messages," *A Different Mountain* (1971) and *Private Speech: Messages 1962–1971* (1971), which he combined into "Messages" (published in the present volume), and his satiric send-ups of French Surrealism under the pseudonym of Georges Zuk, *Georges Zuk: Selected Poems* (1969), *Georges Zuk: The Underwear of the Unicorn* (1975), and *Zuk* (1982).

As an art critic for the *Victoria Daily Times,* as a member of the Limner artists' group, and as a collagist in his own right, he became well known in Victoria's visual-arts community, with one-man shows in Victoria in 1966, 1968, and 1980. His Thursday night open houses were famous meeting points for writers and artists. An inveterate collector of 78-rpm records (four thousand discs), rings (over ninety), books, art, and spiritual objects (hundreds), over time Skelton made his house at 1255 Victoria Avenue a living museum. In all of this work, he was supported by his wife, the calligrapher Sylvia Skelton (née Jarrett), and with her raised three children, Nicholas, Alison, and Brigid. In the 1970s, he accepted the Wiccan faith, and his work as a healer came increasingly to dominate the imagery of his poetry and his life. From the early 1970s, his close friend, the poet Charles Lillard, collaborated with him at *The Malahat Review,* accompanied him on his flea market expeditions, and helped edit his *Collected Shorter Poems* (1981) and *Collected Longer Poems* (1985).

Skelton's effect upon his students was legendary, and many of them went on to become his friends and leading Canadian writers in their own right. In his last dozen years, he wrote increasingly in classical forms and metres, and the last book he completed before his death, *The Shape of Our Singing* (published posthumously in 2003), was an encyclopedia of the verse forms of the world, with a poem written to illustrate each one.

Robin Skelton died peacefully in the presence of his family on August 22, 1997, with the wish to be remembered, above all, as a poet. He was predeceased by his son, Nicholas, in 1994, and followed by his wife, Sylvia, in the fall of 1998. Skelton is survived by his two daughters and two grandsons, who live in Victoria, and by his hundreds of students. He lives on in them all.

ABOUT
HAROLD RHENISCH

Harold Rhenisch was born in Penticton, British Columbia, in 1958 and was raised on an orchard in the Similkameen Valley. On first leaving the farm, he took up Shakespearean acting, playing Puck in *A Midsummer Night's Dream* (1975), before settling into poetry. He studied with Robin Skelton from 1978 to 1980, at which time Skelton selected him for his anthology *Six Poets of British Columbia* (1980). Skelton selected poems from five unpublished manuscripts to publish Rhenisch's third book of poems, *A Delicate Fire* (1989). In the spirit of Zuk, Rhenisch published a long poem entitled *In the Presence of Ghosts* (1993), which starred Skelton and Ezra Pound bantering in Hades. Rhenisch has also edited Skelton's posthumous volume of poetry, *Facing the Light* (2006), and published an elegy, "The Magician," in his volume *The Blue Mouth of Morning* (2000), which Sylvia Skelton read to Robin only hours before his death, and which was read at his memorial service in 1997.

Rhenisch has published nineteen books, including poetry (a dozen volumes, including *Living Will* in 2005, a translation of William Shakespeare's sonnets into contemporary, erotic English), fiction, creative non-fiction, translation, and literary criticism. He is a recipient of the *Arc Poetry Magazine* Poem of the Year prize (2004), the Critic's Desk Award for best feature review of poetry (2003 and 2005), the British Columbia

& Yukon Community Newspapers Association Prize for Best Arts and Culture Writing (1996), and *The Malahat Review* Long Poem Prize (2005 and 2007). He lives in Campbell River, British Columbia.

ACKNOWLEDGEMENTS:
A BLESSING OF FRIENDS

This volume was the labour of many. Charles Lillard helped prepare *The Collected Shorter Poems* (1981) and *The Collected Longer Poems* (1985). Without him, this work would have been incomplete. Robin Skelton's daughters, Alison and Brigid, spent days with me, searching for their father's missing last manuscript, *Facing the Light*, of which I had heard by chance during a conversation with Vancouver publisher Ron Hatch. John Barton, editor of *The Malahat Review*, encouraged me to undertake the project and provided me with vital background material. Without his tenacious patience, persistence, gifted editorial eye, and enthusiasm, this volume would have taken years longer to complete. Peter A. Crowther of Easington, East Yorkshire, generously assisted me with additional biographical material on the shortest of notice. Tim Inkster of The Porcupine's Quill was immediately and genuinely enthusiastic about the project; his unwavering support gave me the energy to continue sifting through a large mass of poems. My greatest debt, however, goes to Seattle poet James Gurley without whose enthusiasm, tirelessness, clarity of vision, and perceptiveness this volume would have been only a shadow of what it has become. James helped select and organize material, helped me to clarify and refine many of my selections, provided invaluable advice on the organization of several sections of the book, and did the backbreaking work of creating the appendices and table of contents. This book has been the work of many.

APPENDIX 1:
ORIGINAL SOURCE INDEX

Begging the Dialect: Poems and Ballads (Oxford University Press, 1960)
    Begging the Dialect
    Land Without Customs

The Dark Window: Poems (Oxford University Press, 1962)
    Alison Jane Skelton
    The Woman

A Ballad of Billy Barker (Morriss Printing Company Chapbook, 1965)
    A Ballad of Billy Barker

Selected Poems 1947–1967 (McClelland & Stewart, 1968)
    Night Poem, Vancouver Island
    Quaternion
    The Ball
    On the Eve of All Hallows

The Hunting Dark (McClelland & Stewart, 1971)
    A Chain of Daisies

Timelight (McClelland & Stewart, 1974)
    Burning Sticks, Mallorca
    The Circumcision
    Overture
    Robert Graves in Deya, Mallorca
    Clare Abbey
    Woodtown Manor, Dublin

Because of Love (McClelland & Stewart, 1977)

    The Gift

    The Hearing

    The Resolution

    By the Lake

    Suppose

    Erosion

    The Separation

Landmarks (Sono Nis Press, 1979)

    Landmarks

    Wood

The Collected Shorter Poems 1947–1977 (Sono Nis Press, 1981)

    The Waking

    A Son Sleeping

Limits (The Porcupine's Quill, 1981)

    Flux

    In This Poem I Am

    Back Again

    Limits

    Kinship

    Triptych

    Heritage

    House Tour

The Collected Longer Poems 1947–1977 (Sono Nis Press, 1985)

    Messages

Distances (The Porcupine's Quill, 1985)

    Marigolds

    Prayer Before Birth

    Palimpsest

    Your Mistake

Openings (Sono Nis Press, 1988)
    Openings
    A Leaf of Privet
    Don't Get Me Wrong
    Making a Poem for Christmas

Popping Fuchsias: Poems 1987–1992 (Ronsdale Press, 1992)
    To Norman Nicholson

The Edge of Time: Poems and Translations (Ronsdale Press, 1995)
    The House

Three for Nick (Pharos Press Chapbook, 1995)
    Letter to Nicholas

One Leaf Shaking: Collected Poems 1977–1990 (Beach Holme Publishing, 1996 and 2000)
    Names
    Everything

Facing the Light (Ekstasis Editions, 2006)
    For William Stafford
    Death
    24.iii.88
    Autobiography

APPENDIX 2:
SOURCES FOR PERMISSIONS

Wrestling the Angel: Collected Shorter Poems 1947–1977 (Beach Holme Publishing, 1994)

> Begging the Dialect
> Land Without Customs
> Alison Jane Skelton
> The Woman
> Night Poem, Vancouver Island
> Quaternion
> The Ball
> On the Eve of All Hallows
> A Chain of Daisies
> The Circumcision
> Overture
> Clare Abbey
> Woodtown Manor, Dublin
> The Gift
> The Hearing
> The Resolution
> By the Lake
> Suppose
> Erosion
> The Separation
> The Waking
> A Son Sleeping
> Robert Graves in Deya, Mallorca

One Leaf Shaking: Collected Poems 1977–1990 (Beach Holme Publishing, second edition, 2000)

    Landmarks

    Wood

    Flux

    In This Poem I Am

    Back Again

    Limits

    Kinship

    Triptych

    Heritage

    House Tour

    Marigolds

    Prayer Before Birth

    Palimpsest

    Your Mistake

    Openings

    A Leaf of Privet

    Don't Get Me Wrong

    Making a Poem for Christmas

    Names

    Everything

    Burning Sticks, Mallorca

The Collected Longer Poems 1947–1977 (Sono Nis Press, 1985)

    Messages

Wordsong: Twelve Ballads (Sono Nis Press, 1983)

    A Ballad of Billy Barker

Popping Fuchsias: Poems 1987–1992 (Ronsdale Press, 1992)

    To Norman Nicholson

The Edge of Time: Poems and Translations (Ronsdale Press, 1995)
    The House

Facing the Light (Ekstasis Editions, 2006)
    For William Stafford
    Death
    24.iii.88
    Autobiography
    Letter to Nicholas